ROUGH WILDERNESS

ROUGH WILDERNESS

THE IMAGINARY LOVE POEMS
OF THE ABBESS HELOISE

Rosemary Aubert

Remy Aubert

*To Eve and Donald
with best wishes,*

Remy

QUATTRO BOOKS

The publication of *Rough Wilderness* has been generously supported by the Canada Council for the Arts and the Ontario Arts Council.

Cover design: Diane Mascherin
Author's photograph: Douglas Purdon
Editor: Allan Briesmaster
Typography: Grey Wolf Typography

Library and Archives Canada Cataloguing in Publication

Aubert, Rosemary
    Rough wilderness : the imaginary love poems
of the Abbess Heloise / Rosemary Aubert.

ISBN 978-1-926802-41-1

    1. Héloïse, 1101-1164--Poetry. I. Title.

PS8551.U24R69 2011   C811'.54   C2011-900537-9

Published by Quattro Books Inc.
89 Pinewood Avenue
Toronto, Ontario,
M6C 2V2
www.quattrobooks.ca

Printed in Canada

To my husband, Douglas Purdon

Contents

Heloise and Abelard were scholars who lived in twelfth-century France. They met when Abelard, already a renowned philosopher and teacher, was asked by Fulbert, Heloise's uncle, to teach his exceptionally bright niece. Heloise was sixteen years younger than Abelard. They were both virgins.

The two fell passionately in love, a love that threatened to ruin Abelard's career in the church. He wanted to marry Heloise, but she refused, offering to become his mistress in order to save his reputation as a philosopher. Enraged by proof of Abelard's treatment of Heloise, Fulbert arranged to have the philosopher castrated.

They did marry, however, but Abelard soon decided it was best for both of them to take holy orders. They lived apart as nun and priest for the remainder of their relatively long lives. This suited Abelard. Heloise never fully came to grips with it.

Abelard founded the Paraclete monastery, which he turned over to Heloise. Her efficient running of the abbey made her one of the most admired women of her time.

Abelard, an arrogant and stubborn man, suffered lifelong setbacks in his career. His ill-fated love for Heloise probably robbed him both of sainthood and of the fame once considered irrefutably his due. Her ill-fated love for him, however, lifted Heloise from obscurity and made of her a symbol of the obstinacy of a strong woman's heart.

MATINS

First bell sings, first bird.
August: cold. December: cold.
In darkness I dream.
A sweet songster is coming.
First prayer: Send him to me.

When I was thirteen,
spring came like a peddler
along the road to our house
bringing lemons from the south,
warm herbs,
stories of the desert and the sea.

When I was thirteen
spring came like music,
a svelte *trouvere*—
birdsong in the cloister branches.

My girlish hopes would wing then
like swallows returning
from the southern sky.

What did I pray for?
What did I half expect?
That the stiff linen the household ladies
sewed into my gowns
would turn to silk.
That Fulbert my uncle would let me
dine at his table
instead of with my nurse.

For jewels.
For permission to wind my braided hair
thrice about my head.

For more books
and enough candles to read them
late into the night.

To travel across the channel to England
and over the mountains to Rome.

And for a man.
Young, with all the power of spring in his limbs,
the face of nearly a saint—
but not quite.
Handsome, ardent, knowing.
Knowing.

One spring,
many years later, it seemed,
you came,
sweet troubadour,
your lean body scented with southern herbs,
your tongue a book
of such secrets.

When I was thirteen,
I knew not what I asked.

SEX BETWEEN VIRGINS

Unseemly
for a maid to wonder,
but I do:

Who
will teach me what
I need to know?

Not
the nuns who braid my hair
and twist a flower there

as if
to tempt a groom.
And not Fulbert.

He
must be a virgin, too
or else he lies.

And not—
heaven forbid—
the priest, who'd read

a list
of evil sins
out from some book.

Look,
if reason reigns
as Fulbert claims

then
I should work
to puzzle these things out.

Some element of woman.
Some part of man.
And love somehow.

If so, then here.
If here, then he.
If he, so I ...

Unseemly
for a maid to ask,
and yet I must:

If there were never
sex between virgins,
would there be virgins?

FULBERT

Some say that Fulbert my uncle
was my father.

Some say he groomed me for himself,
watching, waiting, hoping as old men hope
that I would grow into a woman
while he was still a man.

Some say he rescued me,
found me in a basket by the Seine
like Moses in the silky reeds.

Some say he bought me,
brought me to Paris
to scrub his floors and cook his meals.
The more fool he.

When I grew and I spoke and he saw
that I was as smart as he,
whatever else was planned
was off.

Some say he made me.
Some say he broke my virgin spirit,
then my soul.
Some say he robbed me, raped me, ruined me,
put me on the road to Hell.

I say he brought Abelard.

Enough.

Fulbert showed me a book. It said *agape* means love for
    everyone.
It said *philia* means love for a brother.
It said to love is to give.
It said the love gift of God is the Body of Christ. The body.
God.
Fulbert showed me this book, saying I'd understand it all
    someday.

Someday!
I thought, *My love will never belong to everyone!*
Not the love of God for me nor mine for God,
not the love of a brother.
Not my body,
even if that was mine to give.

Eros is the name of the love the body can give.
Eros is the love I'll understand someday.
Eros is the love of a body for a body.
Eros is the beginning of everyone.
Eros knows nothing of a brother.
Eros, too, is a gift of God?

What is not a gift of God?
And what, besides my body, did I have to give?
Charitas. Alms for the poor man. My brother.
I'd want to give myself to a husband someday,
wouldn't I? Fulbert's book said a nun, like the Lord, gives
    herself to everyone.
But not her body.

I knew from the start my body was not a nun's body.
Nor a body I could give to God.
But everyone
in the end gives God what God wants them to give.
Charitas is the sacred love of free giving. Someday
I'd give that even to Abelard, my brother.

But he was not my brother
the day he claimed my body.
He was not what he would someday
be: the gate between me and God.
He was what I had to give
to gain the love that belongs to everyone.

Everyone *Charitas* my brother.
Give *Eros* my body.
God *Agape* my love. Someday.

PRIME

Dawn breaks. I awake.
From somewhere my uncle speaks.
He says, "Abelard."
The name flutters past stone walls.
Dove in the cave of my heart.

HELOISE ENCOUNTERS ABELARD IN THE MARKETPLACE

What might *I* become to such a man?
I heard him speak to the merchants of madder and woad.
"The root," he said, "distills a beauty greater than the flower."
Smiling, he held a yellow blossom up to me.

I heard him say to the merchants of madder and woad,
"Consider this small, plain bloom, this rough, twisted leaf…"
Smiling, he held the yellow blossom up to me.
"You mock me, sir," I dared. "I am not a flower."

"Consider this small, plain bloom, this rough, twisted leaf…"
I plucked the ugly yellow thing, wrenched it from his grasp.
"You mock me, Abelard," I swore. "I am not a flower."
I thrust the bloom toward his handsome, joking face.

He plucked the ugly yellow thing, wrenched it from my grasp.
"The root," he said, "distills a beauty greater than the flower."
I cast my virgin eyes toward his handsome, joking face.
What flower might *I* become with such a root?

LOOKING DOWN FROM OUR WINDOW ONE EVENING, I GLIMPSE ABELARD IN THE STREET

I see a man who makes a white bear dance.
I see a juggler toss a golden ball
that hovers in the air, stops dead before it starts to fall
as though a wizard freed it from a trance.
I watch them set and reset games of chance
while blazing torches light the conjurer's stall
and avid gamblers caught up in the thrall
ignore the passing timbrels, miss the horses' prance.

More rapt than wagerers, though, are those young men
who follow Abelard from road to stair
and back, as chicks will follow mother hen.
They don't look where they go, nor do they care.
I think they'd blindly enter Satan's den
if Abelard were there …

ABELARD PERFORMS FOR THE CROWD

Your glance makes me the envy
of all other women.
Your strong fingers on the lute,
your tongue around my name,
your eyes seeking mine alone
the way pirates seek the ship's jewels...

What woman would not rather be me
than herself?

Your numberless kisses hidden from the sun,
your hungry embrace sheltered from the moon,
your whispered adulation at my ear
like a breeze freshening the stars...

What woman would not rather be me
than herself?

To be the subject of your song
makes me famous.
To walk at your side
renders me beautiful.
To speak with you,
I am a philosopher.
To love you,
I am most fully
most wonderfully
myself.

What woman would want to be
anybody else?

LOVE WITHOUT BOUNDS

Sea without shore
wild birds circling forever
at the edge of the world.

Sky without cloud
infinite blue curling back on itself
like a song's repeating refrain.

Fields of grain with no fence.
Meadows of grass
with no borders of fragrant herbs.

Forest in which the trees
form canopies
over vast stretches of smaller trees
ad infinitum.

Eternum.

Love without bounds I offer,
myself becoming nothing but what I feel,
my feeling nothing
but the endless joy
of contemplating you.

"FOLLOW, FOOLISH GIRL," HE SAYS, "FOLLOW ME."

Leave loved ones. Leave hearth.
Throw away your thralldom. Thrust manacles aside.
As Nautilus nudges out from his niche
on slippery slime, squeeze free of your chambers.

Now slipping also: the silver moon.
So come with cunning; come fast.
No ear need hear, no eye behold
how you flee, harlot, how you hide.

Love follows love like a stream
gripped by gravity, gaining force,
bubbling from brook to the briny
embrace of the empty sea. Escape.

Liquid seeks liquid. Blood lust.
Maid's tears. Mother's milk. Rain
raging down like a river. Run.

LINEAGE

Abelard's father announced one day
that he would become a monk
and informed Abelard's mother
that she would become a nun.

The father was powerful, a noble.
He moved as the winged horse moves,
fast and away and oblivious
of the wild elements and the pull of earth.

The domain of the father was various.
His seas were pregnant with schooners and barques.
His coffers burst from their weight of gold and gems.
His fields complained of their burden of wheat.

The son is powerful, too.
Full of promise, blessed with bounty.
Touched with glory
now and in the time to come.

Who is scion of noble is noble.

Not like me,
an orphan and a dame.

When Abelard speaks,
sometimes I listen
and sometimes I dream.

Asleep.
Like my own humble father
safely adrift
in the small stone boat
of his grave.

TERCE

Abelard reading
touches each stiff page like silk.
Light kisses his hair,
flows on his skin like sweet milk.
Window light. Firelight. My light.

MORE TOUCHING THAN TEACHING

The day he taught me the difference
between a codex and a scroll,
he slapped me.
His palm was cool against my cheek:
wind from the north,
a leaf wet with rain.

A master's right is to hit the recalcitrant,
but I was a girl
and he shocked himself as well as me.

Codex—bound pages, Abelard.
Scroll—
the roll of parchment along such fingers!
Was it I who reached first
across the skin of some dumb dead lamb
to touch the skin of his wrist?

One afternoon, he read Aristotle.
His voice, like the cooing of doves,
slipped the stone walls and
flew across the rooftops of the town.
In the streets below
his other students gathered
waiting for Abelard
to be finished with me.

But I wasn't finished with him.

I took the book away,
took his face between my hands
and kissed the lips
that Reason claimed her own.

Beneath my palm
a small vein throbbed in his jaw.
I shivered and kissed him again.

Old Aristotle turned in his grave.

In the cemetery of Père Lachaise
somebody walked on mine.

Heloise is a lily. What Abelard wants is a rose.
With nectar, not perfume, is how desire grows.

Between sweetness and passion—what fight?
Wear the crimson, discard the white.

I sought the day. Now I trade it for dark.
Away with dove's coo. Welcome wolf's bark.

Could I draw him with passion, then pull a trick—
Hide love like a needle in the farmer's hayrick?

Yield like butter, then resist like the skin
of the apple that tempted Adam to sin?

Give him heaven but promise the pleasures of hell?
Be lily *and* rose. Could I love *that* well?

LOVE

I knew the moment you began to love me.
I knew the instant your lust
turned to something else less sinful,
more dangerous.

On the table between us
lay open a volume of Cicero.
Your hand was not on that book
but beneath the wool of my bodice
and the fire in the room
was not from coals or wood.

Outside, the short day
gave up its swift weak light.
But there was light enough
that when I gazed into your eyes,
I saw there
not logic, not contempt, not curiosity,
not the half-shut shade
of animal desire,
not even longing
not even the loss
of an innocence neither of us knew you had
until that moment.

What I saw
was an image of myself
and I knew
that from that hour
you would never look out
at the world again
without somehow looking
through me.

AS SHEBA TO SOLOMON I—THE ARRIVAL

"Only the woman he had slept with could reduce to folly Solomon, wisest of all men..."
                    —Heloise, translated by Betty Radice

Pierre precieux, my Solomon, my strong, my wise.
I come to you as Sheba came. These gifts:
The four precious stones: Emerald, Ruby, Sapphire, Diamond.
The spices: spikenard, mace, long pepper, grains-of-paradise.

I come to you as Sheba came. These gifts:
Gold. My secrets. The questions I dare ask no other man.
The spices: spikenard, mace, long pepper, grains-of-paradise
that cut our tongues, keep us awake, until we choose to sleep.

Gold. My secrets. The questions I dare ask no other man—
"What color is the truth?" "How bold is God?" "How love?"
    "How die?"—
that cut our tongues, keep us awake, until we choose to sleep.
If you can answer, Pierre precieux, one other gift: Myself.

"What color is the truth?" "How bold is God?" "How love?"
    "How die?"
The four precious stones: Emerald, Ruby, Sapphire, Diamond.
If you can answer, Pierre precieux, one other gift: Myself.
Pierre, precieux, my Solomon, my strong, my wise.

AS SHEBA TO SOLOMON 2—THE JEWELS

A string of emeralds buys both queen and realm,
and a pigeon-blooded ruby nets a wife.
The devil's totems shine with diamonds rife,
and sapphire's star guides sailors at the helm.

A pigeon-blooded ruby nets a wife,
but wife is not what I would be to thee.
As sapphire's star guides sailors at the helm,
I would guide your spirit sweet and free.

No, wife is not what I would be to thee,
but lover wild as jewels' splintered light;
and I would guide your spirit sweet and free—
hard beauty fracturing the blackest night.

Yes, lover wild as jewel's splintered light,
though devil's totem shine with diamonds rife—
hard beauty fracturing the blackest night.
No string of emeralds needed, queen, nor realm.

When spikenard's oil squeezes sleep from foul valerian,
mace surrounds the nutmeg in its tough embrace and
grains-of-paradise come over Africa by caravan
like long-pepper to burn the virgin tongue.

Mace surrounds the nutmeg in its tough embrace as
I would have you cover me, yielding and unyielding
like long-pepper that burns the virgin tongue
to teach sweet pain—thus power, endurance, will.

I would have you cover me, yielding and unyielding,
strong against your weakness, weak against your strength
to teach sweet pain—thus power, endurance, will,
that we might both become one taste in one soft mouth.

Strong against your weakness, weak against your strength,
grains-of-paradise come over Africa by caravan,
that we might both become one taste in one soft mouth
when spikenard's oil squeezes sleep from foul valerian.

Sheba brought Solomon gold as the sun brings gold to gold,
a surfeit: he made bed posts of it and chamber pots.
He lay in a bed of gold and made a circle in which gold sat like
    God.
So much gold that gold became ballast and sank the ships at sea.

A surfeit: he made bed posts of it and chamber pots,
which is the gold a monk would laugh at, a monk like Abelard.
So much gold that gold became ballast and sank the ships at sea
would amuse the canon of Notre Dame, who considers gold but
    dross.

The gold a monk would laugh at, my Abelard,
is the gold that tastes of nothing, that mixes with nothing.
This amuses the canon of Notre Dame, who considers gold but
    dross
unless it is the mind's gold: light and weight and truth.

The gold that tastes of nothing, that mixes with nothing,
that makes a bed of gold, makes a circle of gold in which gold
    sits like God?
No. It is the mind's gold—light and weight and truth—
that Sheba brought to Solomon, and I, my love, to you.

This is the only secret I told Abelard:
that the heft of him was like bread or earth
or the heavy fall of cloud at the bottom of the sky
on a day that promises thunder and the white heat of lightning,

that the heft of him was like bread or earth,
that his hand on my skin melted me
on a day that promised thunder and white heat,
that I knew my fall like Eve knew hers,

that his hand on my skin melted me
into the pool of lava at the centre of the earth,
that I knew my fall like Eve
and fell anyway—ate the apple, drank the grape of sweet forgetting;

into the pool of lava at the centre of the earth
under the heavy fall of cloud at the bottom of the sky,
I fell—ate the apple, drank the grape of sweet forgetting.
This is the only secret I told Abelard.

SEXT

Startled, he awakes.
"Why are we sleeping at noon?"
"I'll love you always."
The midday bell sounds again,
flushing ravens from their perch.

AUBADE

I awake and turn to find you beside me.
I reach.
I touch.
Your skin is the tender membrane that holds the magic apple's
                bittersweet red seed captive.

I reach.
Chinese apple. Pomegranate.
Your skin is the tender membrane that holds the magic apple's
                bittersweet red seed captive.
I taste.

Chinese apple. Pomegranate.
I would drink you, eat you.
I taste.
Adam am I or Eve in the forbidden garden?

I would drink you, eat you.
I touch.
Adam and Eve sleep in the garden.
I awake.

PHASE

To taste his skin was to drink the milk of the moon.
I would touch him
as no nun touches any sacred thing,
no bowing, no humility.
What does the tongue know of begging for pardon
when it is not wordmaker but whip?

Thus I would please him—there—and oh yes—there,
and he would arch his heavy body up
into the blue light that fell across our bed
hour after hour
always.
It was one of his evil tricks
that whenever I lay with him
the moon shone full
regardless of its phase.

But I never noticed then, except to say
"Your skin in the blue light is milk—
oh my victim, oh my sweet tongue's sweet!"

MEN LEAVING ARE LIKE THAT—VIEW FROM A WINDOW

When they leave
a shower of gold falls before them
and behind.
Their brief and seldom tears turn birdsong,
wing free above the glistening horizon.

How light is the step of a man
who has recently relinquished his lover—
all clean he is,
blithe dancer in the fresh supporting air.

When they leave
sun smiles a blessing.
It never seems to rain
on a man who is walking away.

I hate the dancing nonchalance,
the quick forgetting,
the way he has
of never glancing back.

When a man goes, he goes
sometimes to return

and sometimes not.
As long as the sweet road rises
to his sure step,
what cares he which?

FIRE

More than once when he had me
I opened my eyes
and saw the devil head-on.
The room's low light
glinted off his red beard.
Hellfire.

And his deep grunt of pleasure
drove through the active hour.

Though he took me only in the city,
when that cry broke his lips
I could sense the conies and foxes
of the northern wood
prick up their little ears.

To lie with a man
who can't look you in the eye
is to take the tongue of Satan
into your eager mouth.

Everything gathers into that moment
the way heat gathers into a flame—
one red flaring instant against
all the remaining dark.

ABELARD WRITES DOWN HIS PLAN
FOR AN ABBEY IN THE WILD

My lover dreams of abandoning cities,
of ultimate triumph among the trees.
I watch his half-hidden eyes
as he plans the building of stone walls,
the rise and curve of a road through the wood.

My lover thinks
that the power of mind over wilderness
is not architecture
but cognition.
That nature is kind.
That man can live pure in the wild.

So be it.

Also true:
that he turns in his eager fingers
vellum pages,
forgetting the lamb
who sacrificed
his skin.

MAIDEN'S SONG

I will marry you, love, not in June
but in November
when the wind is like an old woman's fingers
in my hair.
I will marry you, soft husband
in the cloud cathedral.
And if any angel releases
a hard fall of feathered snow,
it will be Lucifer defrocking.

Let the ice that rims the morning fountain
lend color to the bride's cheek
as she washes.

Let dead leaves clacking on the trees
sing wedding march.

Let whatever old priest dares
lead us in these vows.

Marriage has naught to do with love, Abelard.
Except that you ask it of me.
And I—your gray-winged bride:
dove, pigeon, gull, seraphim—
obey.

From this day forward, my betrothed,
all song stops at the back of the throat
where tears freeze
and dam these promises.

HELOISE LEARNS RED TO BLUE

For blue we use woad.
But Abelard taught me
about indigo.

He said it's made by magic,
that the sweet red flowers
of the indigo plant
turn to pods
that the stems turn to reeds
that the reeds foam and ferment
that the foam distills
to some white liquid that turns blue in the air.

These things are not clear to me
despite all Abelard's fine words.

All I remember is this:
His strong fingers lifted a quill,
he dipped it in a well of red
and drew a little flower.

"See this?" He pointed to the crimson bloom.
"Yes."
"And this?" Outside our window the deep blue sky.
"Yes."
"One," he said, "by alchemy becomes the other."

He smiled. A riddle. A joke.

All I can remember is this:
Red becomes blue.
The flower becomes a dye.
The student becomes a fool.
Love becomes a lie.

I never used to ponder the truth
that all things change.
Now I ponder little else.

This, too, will change from red to blue.

NONES

One day his tone changes:
water on white stone, not red,
the hot season fled,
river heavy with drowned leaves,
lark fleeing the golden wood.

SOLOMON TO SHEBA

When he grew old, Solomon had seven hundred wives
who turned the old man away from the love of God.
But when he was young—as you and I were young, Abelard,
Solomon promised Sheba whatever she might ask.

I never asked a man to turn away from God,
though I pulled you where I wanted you to go.
Solomon promised Sheba whatever she might ask.
Here's what I ask you: love, more love, love again, love always.

Though I pulled you where I wanted you to go,
you go elsewhere.
Here's what I ask you: love, more love, love again, love always.
Do you say no?

You go elsewhere.
You and I are still young, Abelard.
Do you say no?
When you grow old, will you have seven hundred wives? Or no wife?

The nurse pressed the babe to my breast.
The nurse pressed the babe to my breast.
Night dropped clouds like a shower of gravel.
Night dropped clouds like a shower of gravel.
The babe of the night pressed like clouds.
Gravel dropped to my breast, a nurse shower.

Did I weep for rainbows?
Did I weep for rainbows?
And was there a stone beneath our tongues?
And was there a stone beneath our tongues?
There was I, beneath rainbows
And a stone did weep for our tongues.

That was the night I learned how the ground howls.
That was the night I learned how the ground howls.
How a seed planted sweet bears bitter fruit.
How a seed planted sweet bears bitter fruit.
Bitter the night that howls; how sweet the fruit was!
I planted. How learnèd a seed the ground bears!

The seed of tongues was a babe dropped beneath clouds.
How bitter the night that I planted!
And I pressed rainbows to my breast.
There was a sweet shower for our nurse.
The ground learned how gravel howls.
Did the night weep the way fruit bears a stone?

CUT

When Fulbert heard what Abelard had done,
that he had sent me off to wear the veil,
that he had made a wife into a nun—
his anger knew no bounds. No weights, no scale

could gauge the heft of fury in his heart
nor coin repay the debt of his hard loss.
So Fulbert set himself to gain the art
of butcher, sculptor, cutter of the dross

and wasteful things that clutter this sweet earth.
He cut, and when he did, left such a void
that weeping students sobbed about the dearth
until the victim fled: pained, shamed, annoyed.

In all of this no person stopped to ask
how I, who had so feasted, might learn to fast.

ARROGANCE

Arrogance is a small man in a large cloak.
Arrogance makes popes out of acolytes, saints out of
  popes.
Arrogance is a loud bird in a vast wood.
Arrogance prays for mighty forgiveness.
Arrogance takes its own census and maps its own
  domain.
Arrogance dances on the head of a pin.
Arrogance sleeps with itself and is satisfied.
Arrogance hoards and is smug in its stores.
Arrogance dispenses truth freely.
Arrogance builds walls on its word.
Arrogance loves mirrors.
Arrogance is a peacock.
Arrogance is a king.
Arrogance is a large man in a small cloak.
Arrogance teaches me your name.
And I hold it on my tongue until it melts.

WHAT PEOPLE WILL SAY—A VILLANELLE

Oh may we never love as these two love
nor be as poorly-made a match as they.
So like, yet not alike: a pigeon and a dove.

May no one ever look to us to prove
that fools strive to marry night with day.
Oh may we never love as these two love.

At heaven's gate while angels laugh above
let not our Judge pronounce on us and say,
"So like, yet not alike! A pigeon and a dove."

The man whose will against God's will would move
soon finds that God's will always has its way.
Oh may we never love as these two love.

To make a circle square, the wise men shove
mathematics into magic, which betrays,
so like, yet not alike. A pigeon and a dove

may stay together for a time, then rove
and on the wind each haste from each away.
Oh may we never fly as these two love.
So like, So unalike. The pigeon and the dove.

LEAVINGS

I loved you so much
that when you left a room
I tried to breathe the air
that had been in your lungs.

I loved you so much
that when you put down a cup
I reached to drink from the place
your lips had touched.

I loved you so much
that when you left the table
I tried to lick your spoon.

I loved you so much
that when you left my bed,
I stretched my length along
the warmth you made.

I loved you so much
that when you left my body
I...
Enough of this.

I loved you so much
that when you left me
I became you.
Tried

VESPERS

I hear Vespers clang,
pigeons squirming in the eaves.
My suckling babe screams.
Rough hands push me to my knees.
Abelard orders me, "Pray!"

BUTCHER

As scalpel scrapes flesh from bone
in abbey kitchen
I cut you away.

HIS EYES

If I am to be shriven, I must speak of windows:
the windows of monasteries,
the portholes of the ship of fools.

If I confess, I must admit to
long corridors lit only by candles
of such arrogant purity
that bees would pray to be victim of
that plunder.

The monks that lived in his eyes
moved without shadow,
soul without shell.
To see thought there, to catch traces of feeling
was to watch the smoke of rubbed beads
rise up
to the pillared forehead of the deity.
Scented, seductive, smudgepots
of righteousness.

Where am I?
His eyes were the portholes on an ocean without
horizon.
I confess.
I drowned myself
in the wave always receding
at the blade edge of the sky.

LOSERS

What we are is nothing.

What we could have been!
Oh, my Loss, in lovers runs
the thin blood of kings
the grandiose dreams of white-steeded knights
the prayer of bishops who know no bounds to their
    asking
the wanton disgrace of queens who are careless
yet happy in their fall,
and the ambition of pawns.

What we were?
A large hand cruel across the board
scattered hope piece by piece.

Endgame, my Sorrow, endgame.

WHAT HE'D SAY IF I ASKED HIM

"Yes, I loved you
but I loved so much else:
my sister Denise—her cool hands,
hands meant only, I guess
for Hugh the Stranger.
So then, not those.
Your hands, too, were cool as water
against my brow.

"Besides you,
I loved the April light
across the solitary page:
Aristotle. Augustine.
The unbridled joy of the heavens by day.
Jerome. Ambrose.
And the barren field of night,
lonely begetter of the myriad stars.

"Heloise, I loved reason more than you.
I loved light more.
I loved myself,
though that, I own, was wrong.

"I am become
more like Origen the eunuch than ever I was,
not only in lack
but in my love
of that absence.

"I loved you once.
I love you.
But more, I love God.
All I care for now
is enclosed by the circle
of his unspeakable name."

LOVE AND DEATH

What love knows of the grave
is what the grave knows of love—
nothing.

Lie down with me now, sweet memory
which I refuse to call sin.
I am a nun
but you are my husband
and I will dream of you naked beside me
no matter what prayer crossed my lips
before I lay.

Oh, Abelard, there are things
the years are powerless to diminish.
There was the morning I woke to turn
and take you in my arms,
the hot length of you
burning me into a languorous wakefulness.
Was it summer?
Was it August misting the trees
with lazy, reluctant dawn?
What reluctance more seductive
than your eyes
refusing to open to morning
and thus prolonging our night?

This, like all else, is gone
and it ill behooves an aging woman,
let alone a tool of God,
to dwell on such remembrance.

But still—
I die, Abelard.
We all die
and the grave knows nothing of love.

Come lie beside me
sweet abstraction
sweet idea of what flesh used to be.
Penetrate this mind
that turns full on you,
even after all these years
still open and guilty and glad…

COMPLINE

At the last bell's ring
I turn to find him gone. Shout.
His name in my lungs
won't fly; freezes, jangling, caught
in the belfry of my ribs.

WHAT COST THIS PEARL?

After hard consideration, I have decided
that the knowledge of my loss
is, of course,
a gift of the Lord.

Eternity, as opposed to the fact
that no one walks for long
in the scented bowers of the afternoon
in which blossoms open
like so many perfumed mouths.

I am talking about earth denied for paradise.

The eye is fleeting and soon must tire
of mote-filled golden light
of shades of green that are air and leaf
and water at once.

The skin of the apple
like the skin of lovers
breaks to the tooth
and perishes.

Still, that garden,
the lovers' Eden,
endures. No nun, nor bishop either
fails to measure sometimes
this gain against that loss.

Besides, one may earn a whole heaven of virtue
for a moment's rigorous denial,
so rich is the mercy
we have been taught.

It would be less virtue
should we forget temptation:
the scented wood, the wayward hand,
the slim suspicion
that earth may indeed harbour
little heavens of its own.

It is well for the saintly
to remember these things.

It is what the Lord decrees,
so that we might know the breadth
of this sacrifice
and the cost
of the heaven of our choice.

A LONG ROAD TO A SMALL COUNTRY

"Do you recall by what great circumlocutions we at length reached this slight point?"
        —St. Augustine

The day before the last days, he sets out.
An act of charity. Also, a rout—

Beyond the hills of Cluny's sweet embrace,
across the river Grosne's gentle race,

eight years before his three-score years and ten,
a man unused to ways of other men.

He travels in the arms of younger monks
safe from the eyes of gossips and quidnuncs.

Unable quite to rise, yet he stares out
from his borne litter, turns and looks about

at houses nestled safe on village streets,
at linens hung to dry—his winding sheet?

Along the way the church bells' chimes decline.
From mother house to daughter house they wind.

And he, he thinks, grows lighter as they go.
His soul becoming ghost, his body slow

as fire retreats into an ember's glow
and all the flaring flame that once did grow

becomes at last a single spark that fails.
These things I know: what helps, what holds, what ails

because of what our friend, the Venerable Peter, writes.
He pictures for me all these timely sights.

What he won't say, I also keep to mind.
Things unsaid, too, are words both keen and kind.

It's this: Once the world rushed to Abelard.
Now he is sent away, all access barred.

He used to tell me, "Heloise, know well,
the road to heaven's longer than to hell."

The road to Abelard is now a trail
that leads my own sad mind to no avail

toward that small country where he takes his rest,
looks back with longing to what's lost—the best.

Your world, my love, at last is come to this:
A captive's bed. And from afar—my kiss.

IN PRAISE OF SADNESS

In another country it is the season of the limes.
They say he sits beneath those trees—
an old man with his back to the sun.

Across landscapes made blurry
with too much watching
he looks in the direction of the Paraclete.
This I know
not only from the brief messages
of passing strangers
but also because I feel his old eyes on me.

Abelard, know this:
Love is a hard stone in a soft mouth.
The years of prayer
have worn smooth my stubborn tongue,
but the taste of you
remains astringent as the juice
of that small fruit
you turn and turn
in your idle hand.

In another country it is the season of the young.
Bow to them who, like you once,
now burn to know, to say,
to love without remorse
in the sinless night.

We, my gone love, are both
grown docile in holiness.
I, for now content to know
the direction in which you set your eyes.
And you
content to wash the space between us
with the weak solution
of an old man's tears.

HELOISE CONSIDERS THE DAYS IN WHICH HE LOVED HER
AS SHE WISHED TO BE LOVED

Oh slender reed of a season
bending in the wind of my years,
I have culled you,
chaotic gift of the orderly earth,
and hold you—a frozen lean bouquet.
Dry, perfect, done.
Foil to all further, and therefore lesser
green.

ROUGH WILDERNESS: PRAYER OF HELOISE ON BECOMING ABBESS OF THE PARACLETE

By the work of my reluctant hand, oh God,
I will heave up toward Thee a temple
out of rough wilderness.
And the reeds of the fields,
wanton reeds without plan in their motion,
shall be forced to bow in homage.
Streams in their tough-banked course
shall sing a hard song in Thy praise.
Obdurate rock shall rise to Thy glory,
oh most stubborn Husband.
And I,
moved like all things of nature
by your imperious hand,
shall clothe myself in the wind of this place.
Let wind be the habit that covers me as I pray
at dawn
at night
at every hour in which
my tongue twists itself
around your name.

VIGILS

Ad Deum

I loved him that much
and he got away.

I loved him
and he grew.

I loved him
and he learned.

I loved him
and he looked at someone, something else.

I loved him that much
and he lied.

I loved him
and he died.

I loved him that much
so I looked for love again.

Someplace else.

I love you
and I'm coming.
As soon as I get away.

LOVE WITHOUT BOUNDS

Sea without shore
wild birds circling forever
at the edge of the world.

Sky without cloud
infinite blue curling back on itself
like a song's repeating refrain.

Fields of grain with no fence.
Meadows of grass
with no borders of fragrant herbs.

Forest in which the trees
form canopies
over vast stretches of smaller trees
ad infinitum.

Eternum.

Love without bounds I offer,
myself becoming nothing but what I feel,
my feeling nothing
but the endless joy
of contemplating Thee.

ACKNOWLEDGEMENTS

Thanks to Allan Briesmaster for his excellent editorial advice and for his continuing support of my work.

Thanks also to Don Cullen and to Sandra Rabinovitch, faithful friends and guides.

Other Quattro Poetry Books